Affiliate Marketing

Experience a Paradigm Shift in Affiliate Marketing
through AI-Driven Automation to Achieve
Unprecedented Success

(Affiliate Marketing for Beginners)

Reginald Bartlett

TABLE OF CONTENT

Affiliate Marketing

WHAT DOES IT REALLY MEANS?

Affiliate marketing involves promoting products or services online and earning commissions. You can accomplish this by obtaining relevant products for your niche, linking them in your blog, and receiving rewards when clients purchase through your links.

This commission can be either a percentage or fixed. You earn a commission by selling the Longrich toothpaste in your blog about healthy living.

You can sell related products on your site as well. You blog about cooking and share recipes. You can sell countless cooking appliances or utensils on your site to facilitate recipe preparation.

You can earn a commission by sharing a link that people can use to sign up. When individuals sign up or complete a survey using the embedded link, you receive a commission. The code or coupon provided by the advertiser is solely for your use to enable tracking.

Several factors must be considered to become a successful affiliate marketer.

More traffic means more earnings.

The poor quality of the product may harm your customer's perception.

Trust drives audience to click and buy.

You can earn money as an affiliate marketer when people purchase the product through your recommended link, even while in bed. As an affiliate marketer, it is crucial not to promote scam links to maintain your integrity.

You may also question why an advertising agency would compensate individuals for advertising in this way. Yes, it may be because they spent a lot on ineffective advertising. With affiliate marketing, payment is mostly based on successful sales. Although their earnings per sale may be reduced in the presence of affiliate networks, their total sales will rise.

Clickbank And Small Niche Websites

This approach entails selecting a Clickbank product within a niche that aligns with your personal interests or passions, and subsequently focusing on low-volume keywords that inherently possess minimal competition.

The majority of advice found on the internet regarding keyword targeting suggests that you should primarily concentrate on keywords that receive a minimum of 1000 exact local searches per month. However, it has become exceedingly challenging to locate such keywords with no competition in contemporary times, thereby making it even more arduous to attain a high rank for those terms.

By focusing on low volume keywords, it immediately implies a decreased level of competition (which subsequently enhances their ranking potential), thereby enabling you to maximize your profits.

After identifying a low volume keyword, you will proceed to construct a concise website with ease, requiring only one hour of your time. Efforts will then be made to promote a relevant Clickbank offer, followed by the implementation of fundamental backlinking strategies. As a result, the website will attain a high-ranking position in search engine results pages, attracting consistent and targeted traffic that will enable you to generate a profit.

Some people will say that mini websites don't work anymore, they don't rank, you need to build authority sites and so on but it's actually not true.

Provided that your content is original, your backlink profile remains secure, you steer clear of exact match domains, and diligently follow a few vital measures on your website (all of which are elucidated in the guide), rest assured that Google algorithm updates pose no threat and your website WILL achieve a favorable ranking.

Should you prefer not to partake in SEO, I have meticulously outlined more than 10 alternative approaches for directing traffic to your website, which are unaffected by Google's algorithms. Such measures will ensure the continued security of your websites against any updates made by the said search engine.

From my perspective, when it comes to mini sites of this nature, I hold a preference towards utilizing SEO techniques. This choice stems from the fact that SEO has the potential to attain quick rankings and maintain them over time with minimal ongoing involvement on my part, in contrast to other traffic generation methods that may require a slightly higher level of ongoing effort.

Overview

Difficulty Level: Easy. Cost: $25

Estimated Setup Time: 2 hours.

Number of hours per week: 2 hours.

Possible Monthly Gain: The potential for earning up to $1000 per site may vary depending on the nature of the product, chosen keywords, and commission rates.

Establish several websites to accommodate various products, with a quick turnaround time of 1-2 hours for site creation, enabling the potential to generate a business yielding $5,000, $10,000, or even $20,000 per month.

The Regulations and the Supplemental Details

It is imperative to consistently peruse the detailed provisions in every contract one intends to enter into. Affiliate marketing holds no exception.

The regulations and intricate details of an affiliate program stipulate the permissible and prohibited actions for promoting products on behalf of the respective company.

Furthermore, they provide information regarding the duration of the cookie, the rate of commissions, and the payment schedule, assuming it is unfamiliar to you.

The detailed terms and conditions outline the guidelines for linking to products, utilizing images for promotional purposes, specifying the permissible images, requirements for obtaining permission to promote program-related content beyond the provided banners and ads, as well as the commission handling process in cases of refund requests.

Furthermore, you will encounter regulations pertaining to Pay-Per-Click (PPC) advertisements, which outline the permissibility of employing this technique for product promotion, as well as specify the prohibited use of certain keywords. It is a customary practice for companies to impose restrictions on the usage of their branded terminology, such as their company or product names, in pay-per-click (PPC) advertisements. This policy is in place to prevent engaging in bidding wars with their own affiliates, thereby inflating the costs associated with running ads on their brand names.

PPC marketing presents significant challenges for implementing affiliate marketing strategies, as it requires adeptness in bidding on non-branded terms and effectively persuading potential consumers to align with the intention of making a purchase. The logical course of action would be to place a bid on branded terms, as such keywords are indicative of more active and interested buyers. However, it is typically prohibited to do so.

The fine print typically encompasses a detailed account of the consequences that individuals may face for non-compliance with the company's regulations, ranging from minor penalties and warnings to the most severe outcome, which involves expulsion from the program.

Although rules and fine print may be tedious, it is essential to thoroughly review them in order to have a clear understanding of the expectations associated with each program you intend to enroll in.

Having gained an understanding of the qualities that constitute an exemplary program, let us now delve into the process of locating a suitable program to participate in.

Mastering the Techniques of Achieving Super Affiliate Status

Over the past few years, there has been a notable expansion in the scale of web hosting services. With the entrance of an increasing number of organizations into this industry and their realization of the numerous benefits it offers, the demand for web hosting services has reached unprecedented heights. These patterns seem to be representative of the prevailing trends in present times.

In the year 2005 alone, a total of 38 million individuals successfully established their initial websites on the internet. It is assessed that by 2008, the Web deals industry will top the dollar bank. Furthermore, it is noteworthy that a majority of these websites offer diverse affiliate programs for individuals to select and participate in.

This main method represents a specific element. Finding the appropriate web host for your application has become significantly more uncomplicated at present. The probability of value web facilitating organizations distinguishing themselves from the rest of the industry is anticipated. If we presuppose the completion of this task, it is anticipated that the inept and clumsily executed efforts will persist.

Primarily considering support will be a key factor for individuals when selecting a web hosting provider. It will become evident that conventional advertising will progressively lose its effectiveness. The overwhelming majority would opt for selecting the internet host based on the perceptions and accounts they have encountered. Furthermore, they are hinged upon suggestions put forth and implemented by individuals who have not only made endeavors, but have also yielded fruitful outcomes.

This presents a remarkable opportunity for both web hosting partners and affiliates alike. There are several web hosting options and platforms available, thus eliminating the challenge of selecting the most suitable one.

What strategies can be employed to transform into a successful sub-entity within niche markets by leveraging web hosting?

From a neutral perspective, it is evident that every individual requiring a website necessitates the services of a web hosting company to provide this facility for them. Currently, there is a lack of established driving facilitation services, leading a large majority to rely on recommendations as their primary method of selection. Typically, they acquire it from those who have previously derived advantages from web hosting services.

Given the abundance of hosts providing derivative programs, there exists the inclination to identify the one that you deem most promising for your circumstances. Please take into account the item you intend to promote. Implement them onto the website and verify if they are addressing the same matters in a manner consistent with your own.

When you have been with a single host for an extended period of time without making significant progress despite your considerable efforts, it would be prudent to depart from that host and seek an alternative option. There is no benefit in trying to adhere to one when you would be better off in another. Progress should ensue from that juncture, as you have already encountered the most unfavorable situations.

Give this a shot. If you are experiencing a state of great contentment and satisfaction with your internet hosting provider, we recommend investigating the possibility of their offering an affiliate program in which you may become a participant. Instead of you making the payment, consider reversing the scenario by having them make the payment to you. The process can be simplified by incorporating a subtle affiliation statement, such as 'fueled by' or 'facilitated by,' at the bottom of your webpage, thus establishing your presence in an affiliate business.

Why opt for immediate payment of your web hosting expenses? Seek renumeration by informing acquaintances of your favorable experience with your web hosting provider.

Always bear in mind that when selecting a web hosting provider, opt for the one renowned for its exceptional customer support. Additionally, there are numerous member programs designed to provide assistance. The residual member initiative is also being facilitated. This is the program in which you receive regular compensation for referring a client. This can enable you to achieve a sustained level of income. With unwavering resolve, one can achieve triumph in this domain.

There are numerous specialized markets awaiting the arrival of suitable individuals who can translate their financial aspirations into reality. Having a clear understanding of which one to pursue entails having unwavering confidence in your true abilities and the exceptional results you are poised to achieve.

Web hosting is a niche market that you may explore to generate substantial and consistent income. It is important to bear in mind that achieving success in your endeavor necessitates the investment of time, effort, and perseverance.

The optimum subordinate market has yet to be conceptualized by anyone. Regardless, there are specific individuals who possess the genuine expertise to achieve remarkable success in such a market. It entails acquiring a comprehensive understanding of your target demographic and capitalizing on the potential for financial gain within that specific market segment.

History Of Affiliate Marketing

The notion of compensating a business that has been referred through revenue sharing or commission payments is not a novel concept. Indeed, this concept originated long before the emergence of the internet and the establishment of affiliate marketing. The incorporation of revenue sharing principles into the mainstream e-commerce commenced in November 1994, around four years subsequent to the deployment of the world wide web.

The notion of online affiliate marketing originated, executed, and secured patent approval from a gentleman named William J. Tobin, the individual credited with the establishment of PC Flowers and Gifts, PC Flowers and Gifts was established in 1989 within the Prodigy Network and functioned within this platform for a duration of seven years until 1996. In 1993, PC Flowers & Gifts achieved an annual sales figure surpassing $6 million through utilization of Prodigy Network's services. PC Flowers and Gifts devised a business strategy in 1998 whereby a remuneration structure was implemented, entailing commissions to be paid based on sales, in association with the Prodigy Network.

In partnership with IBM, given its 50% ownership of Prodigy, Tobin ventured into the realm of the internet by introducing a beta version of PC Flowers and Gifts in 1994. Within the span of a year, a commercially-oriented iteration of the PC Flowers and Gifts website was successfully deployed. In addition, the company boasted a network of 2600 online affiliate marketing partners. Upon comprehending the significance of the business model he had initiated, Tobin submitted an application for patents pertaining to tracking and affiliate marketing on January 22, 1996. Consequently, U.S. Patent number 6,141,666 was duly granted to him on October 31, 2000. Tobin went to great lengths to obtain a Japanese Patent (number 4021941) in 2007 and a U.S. Patent 7,505,913 in 2009 for his contributions to the field of affiliate marketing and tracking. In 1998, a merger was undertaken between PC Flowers and Gifts, Fingerhut, and Federated Department Stores.

Cyber erotica emerged as a pioneering force in the realm of affiliate marketing with its introduction of a program that operated on a cost per click basis.

The progression of innovation was furthered by CDNOW, which initiated the BuyWeb program in November of 1994. CDNOW conceived the notion that websites pertaining to music could possibly feature album listings or critiques for potential purchase, ultimately captivating the interest of website visitors. The websites had the capability to provide a hyperlink that would redirect potential buyers to the CDNOW website, enabling them to complete their purchases there. The genesis of this entire concept can be attributed to deliberations held with Geffen Records, a prominent music label. Geffen's objective was to establish the capability to directly distribute their artists' music through their own website. Nevertheless, they were disinclined to undertake the task of developing this feature on their own. Contrarily, they engaged in discussions with CDNOW regarding the implementation of a scheme wherein CDNOW would assume responsibility for managing the orders. It was observed that CDNOW possessed the capacity to establish links from the artist listed on its own web platform to the official website of Geffen. This would allow for direct access to the music page of the artist, bypassing the CDNOW homepage.

In July 1996, Amazon initiated an associate program known as Amazon.com, enabling associates to display textual hyperlinks or banners promoting specific books on their respective websites. The program additionally facilitated their direct linkage to the Amazon home page. When individuals who perused the website of the affiliate clicked on the designated link leading to Amazon and subsequently made a purchase of a book, a commission was awarded to the affiliate by Amazon. Amazon was not the initial pioneer in providing such an inducement through the utilization of the affiliate program. Nevertheless, its program was the pioneering one that significantly gained popularity and eventually served as a blueprint for other similar programs.

In February 2000, Amazon declared that the company had been awarded a patent for specific elements of an affiliate program. The application was duly submitted in the month of June, 1997. This occurred prior to the establishment of the majority of affiliate programs, but subsequent to the inception of notable programs such as PC Flowers & Gifts.com, which submitted its application in October 1994, AutoWeb.com, which followed suit in October 1995, BrainPlay.com/Kbkids.com in January 1996, EPage in April 1996, and numerous additional programs.

Historic Development

Since its inception, the field of affiliate marketing has experienced rapid growth. During the advent of the internet, e-commerce websites were initially perceived as a novelty in marketing. However, they quickly assumed a significant role within the comprehensive marketing strategies of businesses. In fact, for astute professionals, e-commerce grew to become a more substantial enterprise than their existing offline operations. According to a single report, affiliate networks in the United Kingdom generated a sales volume of £2.16 billion in 2006. In the year 2005, the sales projections had circled around the approximate value of £1.35 billion. According to the estimate provided by the research team at MarketingSherpa, the global earnings of affiliates in the year 2006 amounted to approximately US$6.5 billion in commissions and bounties. The sources encompassed a diverse range of industries, including retail, gambling, telecom, education, and travel, as well as various lead generation methods in addition to contextual advertising programs.

In 2006, affiliate marketing witnessed significant popularity within sectors including gambling, file sharing services, retail industries, and adult entertainment. The cellular phone, financial, and travel sectors were anticipated to exhibit the most significant growth among the three divisions. The entertainment/gaming sector and internet-related service sectors, specifically ISPs, trailed closely behind these aforementioned sectors. Currently, a number of affiliate solution providers expect to experience heightened interest from marketers seeking to incorporate affiliate marketing into their marketing strategies, as well as from businesses and advertisers wishing to utilize affiliate marketing as a component of their overall marketing approach.

Web 2.0

Websites and/or services that have embraced the principles of Web 2.0, including blogging and interactive communities, have significantly influenced the domain of affiliate marketing as well. These platforms enabled enhanced communication channels between merchants and affiliates. Thanks to the advent of Web 2.0 platforms, opportunities for writers, independent website owners, and bloggers to engage in affiliate marketing channels have also emerged. Publishers with moderate web traffic opt for contextual ads as a means to display affiliate advertisements on websites.

The manner in which advertisements are presented to visitors by brands, ad networks, and companies has undergone alterations due to the introduction of new forms of media. Consider YouTube as an illustrative case. YouTube content creators are authorized to incorporate advertisements utilizing Google's affiliate network. Due to recent advancements, unscrupulous affiliates are encountering increased obstacles in their efforts to generate revenue. Such advancements possess the capacity to swiftly and effectively discern nascent fraudulent affiliates and promptly notify the affiliate marketing community of their presence.

Varieties Of Affiliate Marketing

Affiliate marketing presents an advantageous avenue for entrepreneurs to accrue income, particularly within the digital realm where the competition is robust.

There exists a plethora of diverse forms of affiliate marketing, each with its inherent advantages and disadvantages.

"There exist three primary classifications of affiliate marketing:

Pay-per-click model, alternatively referred to as CPC or Cost per click. The advertiser compensates the affiliate for their actions of clicking on an advertisement and producing a sale or lead.

Remuneration based on sale performance: This payment structure is alternatively referred to as CPA (Cost per acquisition). The advertiser compensates the affiliate upon successful conversion and sale.

Under the pay-per-lead model, it is commonly referred to as the CPM method, representing the cost per thousand impressions. The advertiser is responsible for compensating for every generated lead, irrespective of its conversion into a sale or lack thereof.

There exist four distinct categories within the realm of affiliate marketing:

The referral marketing model stands as the most ubiquitous and time-honored form of affiliate marketing. This model operates with a customer-centric approach, wherein users are motivated to guide their acquaintances.

Marketing that relies on intermediaries acting as intermediaries between the marketer and the customer. There exist

31

three distinct categories of intermediaries, namely customers, companies, and retailers.

Affiliate networks are typically marketing agencies that collaborate with numerous marketers in order to engage the targeted audience. They offer enhanced oversight and comprehensive data compared to alternative marketing professionals, yet they also impose a commission fee in exchange for their assistance.

The CPA model represents the most recent addition to the roster of affiliate marketing methods listed. This model centers its attention on securing commissions through the acquisition of customers who commit to specific products or services prior to the disbursement of commissions to the affiliate. The most advantageous aspect of affiliate marketing lies in its potential to not only drive traffic, but also to effectively reduce advertising expenses.

The procedure commences with a thorough comprehension of the affiliate marketing product being promoted and the optimal channels through which to market it. Products may exhibit variations in terms of price, commission rates, and target demographic.

Affiliate Promotional Awareness: The subsequent phase in the realm of affiliate marketing entails generating awareness within the target audience that they have the opportunity to earn income by endorsing your services. This can be achieved via various communication channels such as social media platforms, electronic correspondence, and face-to-face presentations, among others.

Crafting Persuasive Sales Copy: When constructing a high-performing website, it is imperative to generate content that aims to convert site visitors into actively engaged customers, primed for business transactions.

Subsequently, it is necessary to select the most suitable content for your website from diverse options such as blogs, e-books, video courses, among others.

The ultimate phase entails creating a roster of prospective clientele through the utilization of complimentary platforms such as Mail Chimp or Aweber. Subsequently, you can employ this inventory to advertise and market your products and services.

Herein, we present additional guidelines for your reference:

Developing a promotional campaign or a dedicated web page featuring superior content and pertinent keywords in order to entice individuals to engage with it.

In order to identify the most effective advertisements or landing pages that pertain to your selected niche, one may explore prominent corporations such as Google Adwords or Bing Ads, or alternatively seek out affiliate marketers who are amenable to freely sharing their advertisements.

Establish your own website or blog.

Develop your customer profiles.

Find affiliates

Seek out commodities or provisions.

Make sales on your site

Enhance the search engine optimization and online traffic of your website

Creating captivating, compelling, and distinctive content for your advertisement or landing page with the intention to persuade and entice individuals to engage with it.

Creating an account with Amazon Associates, eBay Partner Network, Etsy Affiliates, etc., where you can generate links and earn commissions.

PROFITABLE AFFILIATE MARKETING GUIDE

Establishing a robust sales team is a means of enhancing business growth. In the past, the cost associated with establishing one's own sales team was overly burdensome, creating a substantial impediment for individuals involved in product creation. Fortunately, owing to remarkable advancements in online tracking technology, individuals now have the opportunity to not only engage in sales for a diverse range of products and creators, but also to venture into product creation themselves, for subsequent sale.

One can also leverage affiliate technology to establish a sales force capable of generating substantial six or seven-figure sums, all while avoiding the need for employee recruitment. Compensation for your sales force (affiliates) is exclusively based on successful sales transactions. As an affiliate, your earnings are contingent upon successfully generating sales.

It appears to be straightforward, and indeed, it is. Nevertheless, prior to immersing yourself, it is advisable to acquire comprehensive knowledge regarding affiliate marketing. Gaining knowledge about affiliate marketing and exploring the diverse strategies to optimize your financial gains will propel your company to higher echelons, establishing you as the authentic chief executive officer of your enterprise.

In order to achieve profitability in the realm of affiliate marketing, it is imperative for individuals to initially ascertain their specific target market, subsequently locate suitable merchandise for promotion, develop proprietary products, identify appropriate affiliates to market said products, and maintain the motivation of these affiliates. The process commences by appraising and understanding your specialized market segment.

Finding Your Specialization

The initial step to generate income as an affiliate marketer, whether through promoting others' products or your own (ideally both), entails ascertaining the individuals or organizations you wish to collaborate with and determining the specific niche you desire to engage with.

With whom would you like to engage in collaboration?

Engaging in introspection to identify your interests and passions serves as a means of discerning the kind of individuals with whom you aspire to collaborate or offer assistance. If one derives pleasure from the company of particular individuals and possesses knowledge about their aspirations, wishes, and requirements due to being a part of that group, it can be considered a viable approach as it grants already acquired understanding.

Nevertheless, do not allow this to serve as a justification for evading the undertaking of research. As a constituent of your specific target audience, it is crucial to recognize that one's individual encounters are inherently subjective, and the realized outcomes may deviate significantly from initial expectations. In order to facilitate progress, endeavor to concisely articulate the characteristics of your ideal clientele.

Who is currently catering to that specific target demographic?

After establishing a potential target audience, it is advisable to assess the competitive landscape. In light of the circumstances, can this niche prove to be lucrative in the absence of any competition? Certain individuals may suggest opting for niches with low competition. However, it is more prudent to select a niche with a sufficient number of potential customers to fulfill your income objectives, provided that your conversion rate aligns with industry benchmarks.

For instance, assuming you possess a pool of 1000 prospective clients, with your findings indicating a conversion range of 4 to 7 percent, and having the means to effectively reach out to all of these 1000 potential customers, it is plausible that the resulting campaign could generate a maximum of 70 customers. Does your price threshold sufficiently allow for profitability when catering to those 70 customers?

What competencies and offerings do you possess that would be advantageous in servicing this particular market?

Do you possess any specific academic background, professional expertise, or domain-specific know-how that would render you eligible for this role? One does not necessarily require membership in the audience in order to achieve success within a specific niche.

As an illustration, supposing that you have identified a particular market segment that is in need of expert guidance regarding distinct camping-related products that cannot be commonly found, it remains feasible to acquire knowledge about this niche and cater to the target audience, even if you lack personal experience or affinity for camping. Instead of relying solely on personal experience, it is possible that you possess the necessary resources to engage individuals possessing subject matter expertise, compensating them to develop your enterprise.

What distinguishes you?

It is imperative to consistently introspect and evaluate oneself. What sets you apart from your competitors? What unique skills or competencies do you possess that set you apart from others in this specific field? What strategies can you employ to set yourself apart from the multitude? Will you adopt a distinctive approach to the niche compared to others? For instance, in the context of being a business coach, would you adopt a formal or informal demeanor? Irrespective of one's characteristics, individuals will inevitably draw a distinct demographic of viewers that differs significantly from those who do not share similar traits.

Conduct a thorough examination of an Affiliate Network to identify products that specifically target the relevant demographic.

An additional factor to take into consideration pertains to the profitability of the niche that you opt for. It is imperative to evaluate the profitability of the situation by posing the question to oneself. The possession of internet access and one's enthusiasm for a subject does not guarantee its viability as a lucrative niche. The profitability of this venture stems from the presence of an adequately sized target audience with the necessary financial resources to acquire the solutions you develop and provide.

After you have limited your choices, the chief factors to take into account are the potential profitability of your niche concept and your aptitude to proceed, either by acquiring the necessary skills or purchasing them from others. Select a commercially viable market segment that aligns with your personal interest and expertise.

Proper Procedure For Registering An Account On Clickbank

Should you be interested in entry into the Clickbank platform, you have the opportunity to proceed by selecting from a choice of two available options. You have the option of opening either a Clickbank Affiliate Account, enabling you to effectively advertise and endorse digital products of your preference, or a Clickbank Vendors Account, allowing you to directly sell your own digital products.

Clickbank Affiliate Account

By possessing an affiliate account, you gain the ability to carefully select from the extensive array of digital products available within the Clickbank online marketplace, and subsequently market and endorse them. When the product you are promoting is successfully sold due to your marketing endeavors, you are entitled to receive a commission, the percentage of which may vary from 1% to 75%.

Enrolling as an affiliate member entails no financial obligation on your part. There are no associated registration fees or joining fees. In order to become a Clickbank affiliate, it is necessary to possess a valid email Id, a permanent address for the receipt of commission checks, a working phone number for accessibility, and an age requirement of at least 18 years of age.

"To enroll as an affiliate, it is necessary to undertake the subsequent procedures: ⬚

Procede to the Clickbank website and select the sign-up link. ⬚

Please complete the online form with accurate information. It is imperative that you meticulously and comprehensively complete all fields with accurate information. The dissemination of inaccurate information may result in the suspension or withholding of your payment.

Choose an account nickname. When selecting a nickname, opt for one that is easily recollected. It is also necessary to input a password. Please ensure that you select a password that you will easily remember. This is of utmost significance as your chosen identifier and secret phrase hold significant importance for you to gain access. ⍰

Subsequently, it is essential for you to thoroughly examine the Client Contract and proceed to select the appropriate checkbox to confirm that you have duly

perused and comprehended its contents.
⍰

You will be directed to a webpage displaying the message "sign-up not yet complete," indicating that a confirmation code has been dispatched to the email address you provided during the sign-up process.

Open you email. There will be a hyperlink provided, which you are required to select in order to be redirected to a webpage where you will need to input your 8-digit confirmation code. Kindly input the verification code found within your email into the designated section on the confirmation page. Afterward, you will be kindly asked to input the captcha code.

Once you have successfully completed the registration process, you will be directed to the login page.

Clickbank Vendor Account

By possessing a vendor account, you gain the ability to market and distribute a digital product that you personally developed. An initial charge of $49.95 is required to facilitate the promotion of your product(s). One benefit that arises from this situation is the presence of a vast network of affiliates who can effectively promote your product on your behalf. As a result, when your product is successfully sold, you will receive compensation, and this source of income will persist as long as your products continue to be sold.

Regardless of the account option you select, you will be able to benefit from the efficiently operating infrastructure provided by Clickbank. Clickbank provides a secure payment gateway that enables customers to conveniently make payments using their credit cards, eliminating the need for vendors to go through the cumbersome process of obtaining merchant accounts. Additionally, the calculation and disbursement of affiliate commissions are performed by Clickbank, thereby alleviating the vendors' concerns and allowing them to concentrate on generating innovative products. Acquiring a Clickbank account can significantly increase your earning potential, either as a vendor or as an affiliate.

In order to become a Clickbank vendor, it is necessary to adhere to the subsequent procedures:

Please navigate to the official Clickbank website and locate the sign-up link located at the top section of the page.

Please input the necessary data in the designated fields with complete and accurate information.

Choose an account nickname. Make sure that you choose a nickname that you are unlikely to forget. Then choose a password. Please be advised that these items are necessary for the purpose of logging in, so it is of utmost importance that you make your selection judiciously. Your password should possess a high level of security while remaining easily memorable. ▯

You are required to thoroughly peruse and comprehend the Client Contract, subsequently selecting the appropriate box to confirm your comprehension of its contents.

After completing the sign-up process, you will be directed to a webpage indicating that your registration is incomplete. Subsequently, kindly check your email account for the confirmation email dispatched by Clickbank.

Open your email. You will receive an email from Clickbank containing an 8-digit confirmation code along with a hyperlink. Kindly access the provided hyperlink, and it will redirect you to a webpage where you will be prompted to input the 8-digit confirmation code and complete a captcha verification.

You have successfully completed the registration process and will now be redirected to the login page, where you may begin accessing your account.

Regardless of whether you intend to become an affiliate or a vendor, the enrollment process remains consistent. Thus, there is no immediate need to fret over determining the specific account type you must acquire.

Subsequent to creating your account, it will be necessary for you to provide the required details on the designated "My Account" webpage. All of your main account details, including your contact and payment information, are managed within the 'My Account' section.

Please ensure the accuracy and completeness of all provided information, as Clickbank checks will be dispatched exclusively to the address you provide. In the event that there are any inaccuracies present within the provided address, there is a potential risk of non-receipt of your remittances. All tax information will be located on that page as well, therefore it is imperative that you ensure the accuracy of your entries.

Owning a Clickbank account affords you the opportunity to capitalize on the possibilities available to you as either an affiliate or a vendor. By dedicating a modest amount of time, exertion, and resilience, one can effectively amass a satisfactory income from the confines of one's own residence. You have the opportunity to generate revenue through the sale of digital products that you have developed as a vendor, or by engaging in affiliate marketing where you promote products created by others.

The Merits of Affiliate Marketing as an Optimal Income Generation Method for Novices Initiating Their Monetary Pursuits in the Initial Phase

A significant number of individuals lack familiarity with the concept of affiliate marketing. Is it conceivable to generate financial gain from a product for which you have not even contributed to its creation?

How could it be conceivable that generating income through digital means could be so effortless? Theconceptcanbereducedtoitsmostfund amentalformbystatingthatitis sales. You are serving in the capacity of a seller, and any successful sales that you facilitate will entitle you to receive a commission. In this context, you bear resemblance to the sales representatives who engage in door-to-door visits with the purpose of promoting and offering broadband internet services to residential customers.

The primary differentiation lies in the fact that you are not physically traversing between residences. Through the utilization of the internet as your gateway, you possess unrestricted entry to all individuals, as this digital portal grants you unparalleled accessibility to the global population.

As a consequence, instantaneous leverage is acquired, further magnified as you devise strategies to allure customers to your establishment.

The commission structure will exhibit significant divergence from other circumstances, establishing another crucial disparity in this case. In the majority of instances, conventional sales agents can expect to receive a moderate commission on the sale of products or services, typically falling within the range of 5 to 10 percent. As previously stated, the key characteristic of affiliate marketing lies in the assurance that a generous portion, ranging from 70 to 80 percent, of the profits will be awarded to you. Indeed, your perception is accurate: in the capacity of an affiliate marketer, it is often the case that your income surpasses that of the individual who initially conceived and developed the product.

The opportunity to generate income right away, akin to marketing your own product, without the need for substantial upfront investments in the development of an entirely new entity, exemplifies one of the myriad reasons why affiliate marketing engenders great allure as a business model.

Given that you will be engaged in the sale of a product that is already available in the market, you will possess the opportunity to choose an item that has demonstrated commendable performance in terms of sales magnitude. This confers an supplementary advantage. When endeavoring to create a product for the purpose of commercializing it, there exists a likelihood that one may manufacture an item that lacks demand amongst consumers. When promoting a product or service that already enjoys substantial popularity, the probability of such an occurrence happening is considerably diminished.

An additional notable benefit of affiliate marketing lies in its inherent scalability, allowing for seamless expansion or contraction as desired. It is possible to commence generating income through an affiliate program merely hours after developing a solitary web page that effectively promotes the merits of an affiliated product and facilitates its sale. Given this,

Should this be the scenario, there are no impediments preventing you from initiating a new webpage to offer an alternative product for sale. And once again, we encounter an additional page dedicated to the promotion of an alternative product?

The Methodology Involved in Affiliate Marketing

Now that we have addressed that matter, may we delve into a more detailed discussion? What is the precise mechanism of operation for affiliate marketing, and what would prompt a content creator to willingly part with a substantial portion of their own earnings in the first instance?

To commence, let us discuss the various types of content that you intend to market for purchase. Many online marketers classify affiliate products as digital products.

There exists a wide range of alternative options, a selection of which we shall delve into later within the pages of this book. However, at present, our focus will be directed towards that objective. This encompasses items such as digital books, internet-based educational programs, and multimedia demonstrations, among comparable entities. These offerings incur negligible expenses and are devoid of operational overheads.

AFFILIATE MARKETING

Considering the term 'COGs' which stands for 'cost of goods sold,' it is noteworthy that digital products present a highly favorable option for online sales due to their inherent lack of overhead expenses. Consequently, this implies that the originator of the product/service is exempted from incurring any expense for each transaction, enabling them to concentrate on generating profits and subsequently distributing a share of those profits among the other contributors. Additionally, it signifies that they were never obligated to make substantial upfront investments, and it relieves them from the responsibility of overseeing the delivery process.

Hence, it is highly probable that the originator of this digital product personally produced it using either Microsoft Word or a camera, or alternatively, they might have outsourced the production to a third party. In either scenario, their intention would be to generate profits by marketing and selling either the ebook or the course.

Subsequently, it is highly probable that the developer initiated the sale of the aforementioned product either through their personal website or an arbitrary online platform. They will endeavor to generate maximum website traffic with the aim of convincing visitors to make a purchase, ultimately leading to the establishment of their own self-sustaining source of income.

Nevertheless, there exists a finite capacity for an individual to promote, and eventually, their resources will be depleted. Once this milestone has been achieved, a creator may commence the search for affiliations to engage in collaborative efforts, seeking their assistance in the promotion of their products.

As a result of this, the product creator demonstrates their willingness to extend a commission of seventy percent or more to affiliates like ourselves, with the intention of incentivizing our efforts in promoting their merchandise. They express the preference for us to prioritize the promotion and sale of their products over those from other creators with affiliate programs due to their desire to maximize their financial gains.

Although the revenue percentage for the creator's sales has diminished to 30%, it is noteworthy that this still represents an increase of 30% compared to the hypothetical scenario where they would have remained within the market. This is attributable to the circumstance that they would not have withdrawn from the market.

If the seller manages to persuade a multitude of individuals to purchase their books through the assistance of a large group of online marketers, not only will they attain substantial profits, but they will also gain the capacity to achieve far more than they would be capable of accomplishing independently.

In conclusion, both parties stand to gain advantages in this particular situation. The creator effectively generates an additional one thousand sales through their initiative in fostering collaborative partnerships with marketers.

Affiliates are provided with the chance to market a product as if it were their own, thereby retaining a significant portion of the generated profits. They have the capacity to generate an equivalent income as if they were to sell their personal eBook or course, without having to invest effort in creating and managing said products, nor assuming the immense risk associated with such ventures.

More precisely, the mechanism by which this process operates is through the utilization of "affiliate links," which, in turn, operate through the use of cookies.

Once you have identified an affiliate product that you wish to endorse, an affiliate link will be assigned to you. Kindly ensure to incorporate this hyperlink on both your sales page and blog posts, as it is imperative for facilitating product purchases through your designated affiliate link.

When a prospective client activates your affiliate hyperlink, they will initially be redirected to an alternative webpage located elsewhere on the internet. Upon accessing this page, a cookie will be stored on the user's computer to indicate their origin from your website. Henceforth, whenever they make a purchase from that establishment, they shall be identified as your affiliated customer, and the corresponding commission shall be incorporated into your cumulative balance, affording you the liberty to withdraw it at a later juncture, should you wish to do so.

You need to solely promote the product and provide the hyperlink for individuals to access. That leads us to the final outcome

Earning Income Through Your Blog

This chapter is designed to provide comprehensive guidance on the process of monetizing your blog. It will offer you guidance, insights, and methodologies that can be effectively employed to generate income from your newly established website.

The Techniques

Ads utilizing the Cost Per Click (CPC) model

Many bloggers generate revenue from their websites by implementing Cost Per Click advertisements. True to its nomenclature, a Cost Per Click (CPC) advertising system offers remuneration for each instance when a visitor clicks on an advertisement. Adsense, a prominent advertising program offered by Google, currently holds the top position in terms of popularity as a choice for CPC advertising. Google will perform a review of your articles through the implementation of Adsense. Afterward, it will seek out advertisements that are relevant to said articles. Due to the correlation between the advertisements and the content of the blog entries, this advertising approach produces exceptional outcomes.

Please take note: Further details regarding Adsense will be presented in subsequent sections of this chapter.

This system presents numerous advantages to both bloggers and readers. It enables bloggers to generate income through their web-based articles. In addition, it enables readers to conveniently discover and avail the products and/or services that are essential to their requirements.

Advertisement model based on CPM (Cost Per Thousand)

This particular advertising system compensates you in accordance with the quantity of visitors that view the advertisements. The abbreviation "CPM" originates from the Roman numeral "M", which symbolizes the numerical value of 1,000. The revenue generated from this advertising system is expected to be modest in the initial months of your career as a blogger. Nevertheless, once your blog attains considerable traffic, utilizing CPM advertising can substantially augment your financial earnings. Below, I have compiled a list of the most widely recognized CPM networks presently in use:

Adbrite.com

Pulsepoint.com

Casalemedia.com

AdClickMedia.com

Technoratimedia.com

Adify.com

Each of these networks possesses unique advantages and disadvantages. It is advisable to conduct an analysis of each network prior to featuring them on your blog. By following this approach, you can ensure that the CPM network you are utilizing aligns effectively with your specific requirements.

Affiliate Products

In your role as a blogger, you have the opportunity to serve as a mediator between sellers and prospective buyers.

You have the opportunity to establish collaborative alliances with individuals or enterprises that provide products and/or services that are pertinent to the subject matter of your blog. Following that, you will proceed to endorse and promote said products/services through the content featured on your blog. In this arrangement, you stand to generate income whenever one of your readers makes a payment in exchange for the aforementioned products or services.

This advertising system effectively transforms individuals into adept sales professionals. Nevertheless, in contrast to conventional sales personnel, you possess the ability to effectively market a wide array of products and/or services to an unlimited audience, thereby establishing fruitful collaborations with an extensive network of vendors.

Presented herewith are a selection of esteemed affiliate programs that you may leverage for the enhancement of your website:

Flexoffers.com

LinkShare.com

Shareasale.com

CJ.com

E-Junkie.com

Affiliate-program.amazon.com

Panthera.com

LogicalMedia.com

RedPlum.com

MoneySavingMom.com

Coupons.com

MySavings.com

It is advisable that you maintain honesty in each of your recommendations. Provide impartial assessments regarding the merchandise and/or services presented on your blog. For example, you have the option to generate an article wherein you compile the advantages and disadvantages of a particular product for the purpose of enlightening your readers on pertinent aspects of that market offering.

This system functions effectively as it facilitates simultaneous benefits for three parties. You have the potential to generate income through recommending others. Sellers get more customers. In contrast, your readers are provided with valuable information regarding the products or services that could potentially prove beneficial to them. In due course, you will acquire additional knowledge pertaining to affiliate advertising.

Ad Space

Additionally, you may choose to provide advertising space to digital marketers. A myriad of bloggers have attempted this system and achieved success. Selling advertising slots to marketers proves to be extremely effective when deployed within specialized markets. To implement this advertising system on your blog, simply access the official website of www.buysellads.com. That website facilitates the connection between marketers and bloggers.

The Timeframe

Now that you possess the knowledge on how to generate revenue from your blog, it is likely that you are interested in determining the timeframe required to establish a stable and continuous income flow. It is imperative to underline that blogging does not constitute the most expeditious method of generating income. It encompasses an extensive duration." "It entails an extended period of time." "It encompasses a significant time span." "It entails a prolonged timeframe. Even the most proficient bloggers had to endure extended periods of time, spanning several months or even years, before achieving a level of income that met their expectations.

Naturally, if you possess a pre-existing understanding of advertising, content creation, search engine optimization, and other areas pertaining to blogging, you can considerably reduce the duration of the task.

Maximizing the Effectiveness of Adsense Usage

This section of the book will furnish you with sophisticated methodologies. These techniques have been developed to enhance your revenue generated through Google's Adsense program. By implementing these techniques on your website, you have the potential to significantly increase your revenue generated from Adsense, possibly even doubling or tripling it.

It's important to point out that each blog is unique. Even within the same niche, blogs can exhibit variations in their layouts, readership, and content. These factors have a significant impact on the potential earnings derived from the Adsense program. Nevertheless, the methodologies provided here can be of assistance in enhancing your Adsense campaign irrespective of your domain, website design, and existing blog articles.

1. Strategically position advertisements in highly visible locations to capture the

attention of readers. It should be noted that revenue is generated through Adsense when readers interact with the advertisements by clicking on them. Consequently, it is advisable to position those advertisements strategically within the visually appealing sections of your blog. Nevertheless, it is imperative to take into account the overall user-friendliness of your website. If you were to indiscriminately incorporate Adsense advertisements, it is conceivable that visitors could refrain from accessing your blog. In order to optimize the advantages derived from Adsense, it is imperative to acquire a proficient grasp of the strategic placement of advertisements.

2. Deliberately focus on designated sections of your blog posts – Employing this strategy entails identifying and highlighting precise segments within your articles that warrant Google's

scrutiny during the ad selection process. Incorporating this methodology into your blog is straightforward and effortless. One must simply input " " into the system.

Conversion Systems With A Focus On Generating Profit

The subsequent content pertains to an analysis of contemporary conversion systems. These conversion systems are the most recent and sophisticated. These are the prevailing instances. Naturally, I will not feign that this is an exhaustive compilation. That's not the case. Certainly not. On the contrary, these are exclusively the conversion systems with which you are prone to encounter during your internet browsing.

Promotion through a Direct Link

With the utilization of this system, one can essentially generate income by acquiring the designated affiliate link provided by the program and procuring traffic for said link through monetary investment. In a formal tone, you access the Facebook platform, choose a specific image, establish a financial plan, and subsequently input your link into the designated URL field. Pretty straightforward. You are purchasing web traffic and directly redirecting it to your designated link.

Advantages

The primary benefit of this conversion system lies in its ability to efficiently and expeditiously generate traffic. There is no need for you to excessively search for traffic.

Disadvantages

It is possible that you will need to incur significant expenses prior to generating any revenue, if revenue is indeed realized. Extensive experimentation is necessary to refine the targeting parameters for advertising on platforms like Facebook or Google AdWords.

Web Traffic generated from Content-Focused Advertising

With the implementation of this conversion system, you have the ability to generate content. Perhaps you are engaged in the promotion of content on a third-party website, utilizing a financial arrangement wherein you compensate them for its publication. Alternatively, you may operate a content-centric platform such as a blog. Regardless of the circumstances, there is a hyperlink within your content. If individuals opt to click on the provided hyperlink, they will be directed to an alternate webpage within your website designed to promote the affiliated proposition, or alternatively, they will be directed straight to the website of your affiliated sponsor. These links may be in the form of a text hyperlink or they may be associated with an image.

Advantages

One significant benefit of content-based ad traffic is the opportunity to exert substantial influence over the mindset of your visitors. You're not merely presenting an advertisement to them in a strictly binary accept or decline scenario. When it comes to content, it enables you to address their requirements. You are able to capture their attention. You have the opportunity to instill in them a desire to delve deeper into learning additional information about your proposed resolution to their predicament.

You are able to create and establish a unique branding presence directly in front of your customers. You have the opportunity to transmit a wide range of signals and information to enable them to establish a connection between your brand and a specific set of values that they seek in a product.

Disadvantages

Unless you are financially investing in the placement of your article or blog post, the reliability of generating traffic remains uncertain. If you have already attained expertise in generating traffic, then there is no cause for concern in this regard. Nevertheless, if you belong to the majority who may lack proficiency in consistently generating traffic, utilizing content as a means of advertising affiliate programs may not yield favorable results.

Correspondence-Driven Congestion

This holds a special place as my preferred choice. The overwhelming majority of individuals who visit your blog or encounter your content are unlikely to return. Wouldn't it be beneficial to establish a durable relationship with them, thereby ensuring a means of enticing their return to your website, or at the very least, having a method of engaging them to click on an affiliate link? Establishing an email database allows you to accomplish these objectives.

You can enhance the visibility of your mailing list either by means of compelling content or through targeted promotional campaigns using AdWords or Facebook. When people enter their email address, you develop a relationship with them. You can continue to send them updates until a juncture at which they click on a link and make a purchase, or alternatively, they may become fatigued with your electronic communications and choose to discontinue their subscription. Notwithstanding, you possess numerous opportunities to subsequently convert them.

Advantages

One notable benefit of email marketing is the opportunity for multiple touchpoints or interactions with potential recipients. You are not obliged to convert them immediately on the spot. Conversely, you establish a rapport with them. If you present highly persuasive content or captivate them with intriguing material, there is a possibility that they will be inclined to click on a link, resulting in a monetary contribution to your account. An additional advantageous aspect of email list marketing is its capability to facilitate marketing efforts towards customers in a flexible and convenient manner, regardless of time or location.

Disadvantages

The process of accumulating a mailing list requires a considerable investment of time. Occasionally, list marketing can become costly due to the presence of list squatters. These individuals are individuals who willingly subscribe to your mailing list, yet refrain from unsubscribing despite their apparent disinterest in reading your updates. It is imperative to actively monitor and manage these individuals, as failure to do so can potentially result in significant financial implications in the form of mailing service charges. The majority of email systems implement a pricing structure that is dependent on the size of your mailing list rather than the number of individuals who actively engage with your updates. In order to address the issue of list squatters, various email systems, such as AWeber, provide functionality that allows you to identify individuals on your mailing list who have not opened your emails and remove them from the list.

Review Traffic

You have the opportunity to publish a review concerning either the product you are endorsing or another product that is relevant to the product in question. This content garners online visitors since individuals seek reviews prior to making a purchase.

Advantages

The big advantage to review traffic is that it's direct traffic. It is highly uncommon to encounter individuals who lack interest in the subject matter you are reviewing. Why? You are, in fact, evaluating the items under consideration for purchase.

Additionally, if you are endorsing a product that is relevant to the item that individuals are seeking feedback on, you will also receive direct traffic. Why? These individuals possess a direct vested interest in a product that is closely aligned with the product being promoted by you. This is equally satisfactory in comparison to direct traffic.

The objective is to persuade them to reconsider their initial preference for the reviewed product, thereby diverting their attention towards the merchandise you are endorsing. Pretty clever. A prevalent illustration of such review activity that bears some relation to the aforementioned is comprised of reviews pertaining to scams or anti-fraud incidents. In essence, the procedure involves appending the term "scam" or "fraud" followed by a question mark to the name of the product.

Upon perusing the review, individuals come to realize that it presents a relatively impartial assessment of the product they have a vested interest in. However, strategically positioned at either the commencement or the conclusion of the review, you skillfully generate enthusiasm for a related product, asserting its credibility and dispelling any doubts of its authenticity. This particular variation yields significant traffic from search engines, exemplifying its strong efficacy.

Disadvantages

If you focus on a saturated niche, the influx of review traffic will not be advantageous. Your domain has been inundated by fellow marketers. They are receiving the majority of the traffic, leaving only a minimal amount for you. In addition, it is imperative to possess a profound understanding of search engine optimization techniques. If you lack proficiency in the field of SEO, you may still experience some level of website traffic, albeit of an insufficient magnitude to justify your efforts.

Video Traffic

YouTube is a prominent source of web traffic, and it can certainly yield a substantial volume of visitors. This is why a lot of people are creating review videos and then posting them on YouTube. Additionally, they produce instructional videos, commonly referred to as "How To" videos, with the purpose of generating website traffic.

When individuals perform a query within your specific industry and encounter your video content, they proceed to engage with the visual material. Additionally, when you direct individuals to a provided link within the description, they have the ability to access the link and consequently generate traffic to your website or platform.

Advantages

Video traffic holds significant potency, as it is comparatively more feasible to attain a high ranking on YouTube as opposed to Google's search engine. You have a significant likelihood of experiencing higher website traffic from YouTube compared to the conventional Google search engine.

Disadvantage

If the market within your niche is saturated or excessively populated, YouTube may not be a suitable platform for you to consider. Additionally, it may be necessary for you to consider purchasing views for your video in order to establish social validation. The greater the number of views your videos attain, the higher the likelihood of individuals being inclined to click through and watch them.

Exploratory Platform featuring Exclusive Content

This tool entails the development of a search engine that facilitates individuals in accessing and browsing relevant content pertaining to the affiliate offers. Notable illustrations of this phenomenon encompass online platforms dedicated to the reservation of airline tickets and accommodations.

Advantage

You provide greater value in this context. You are not solely disseminating an article containing affiliate links. Alternatively, individuals have the option to compare and contrast various products in order to arrive at an informed decision, or they can seek out specific and detailed information pertaining to a product prior to making a choice.

Disadvantage

One major drawback associated with search platforms that showcase exclusive content is the financial burden it entails. Either you possess the expertise in programming specialized search engines and can execute the task independently, or you will need to allocate a significant amount of financial resources to outsource this project.

Specialized Product Evaluation Platform

Many affiliates have established searchable platforms that provide individuals with the opportunity to peruse diverse product reviews within a specific industry. Subsequently, they may proceed to compare and correlate the various products. This encompasses travel destinations as well as dining establishments.

Review platforms possess significant influence due to the fact that individuals actively seek out specialized information pertaining to services. An exemplary illustration can be observed through the platform of TripAdvisor.

Advantages

One notable benefit of product review platforms lies in their ability to enhance the user's overall experience by providing substantial value. They are not merely acquiring arbitrary knowledge.

They possess the ability to cross examine this information, they have the capacity to scrutinize materials shared by other individuals. In addition, this platform has a tendency to foster a sense of community among its users centered around the content. When individuals arrive at TripAdvisor, such as, they proceed to recount their experiences.

Disadvantage

The production expenses incurred for developing these tailor-made platforms can be substantial. You require specialized programming in order to accomplish this. You are also required to possess a resilient content management system. You cannot solely depend on WordPress to ensure your success.

What Are The Top Affiliate Marketing Platforms?

Affiliate marketing platforms are highly favored by both product merchants and affiliate marketers alike. This is due to their exceptional capabilities and strategic positioning in facilitating connections between buyers of affiliate marketing services (product merchants) and suppliers of affiliate marketing services (affiliate marketers). Consequently, these platforms serve as virtual marketplaces where both product merchants and affiliate marketers can connect, engage, and engage in transactions.

There exist variations among different affiliate marketing platforms. Hence, it is imperative to establish discerning criteria that will facilitate the identification of the optimal affiliate marketing platform for your unique needs. This holds utmost importance in determining the success of your affiliate marketing enterprise.

Parameters for selecting the optimal affiliate marketing platform; "Factors to consider when identifying the most suitable affiliate marketing platform; "Categorization for determining the top affiliate marketing platform; "Standards for evaluating the finest affiliate marketing platform; "Guidelines for ascertaining the most advantageous affiliate marketing platform.

Reputation

Commission percentage

Assortment of products available for marketing Variety of products for promotional purposes Diverse array of products for marketing purposes Selection of products for market distribution Wide range of products for marketing endeavors

Variety of revenue sources

Payment terms

Terms of service

Reputation

The primacy of reputation serves as the primary determinant when selecting an Affiliate marketing platform. A strong reputation is established through upholding high levels of integrity and ensuring exceptional customer experiences. The level of your earnings is greatly influenced by the integrity of your affiliate marketing platform. A disreputable affiliate marketing platform is more inclined to deprive you of your rightful income. You certainly do not wish to exert yourself in vain. You would not wish to miss out on the rewards that stem from your diligent efforts. Reputation is paramount.

Commission percentage

Various affiliate marketing platforms impose varying commission rates on identical products. It is customary for the same product to exhibit varied pricing among different retailers, as per prevailing market dynamics. The percentage of commission is frequently subject to negotiation between the product merchant and the affiliate merchant. Consequently, the commission percentage you will be offered is contingent upon the affiliate merchant's performance and reputation. After compiling a list of esteemed affiliate marketing platforms, namely the top three contenders, you can proceed to derive a comparative analysis of commission percentages, ultimately determining the platform that presents the most attractive commission payout.

Assortment of products for marketing purposes.

Primarily, an affiliate marketing platform functions as a marketplace for marketing purposes. It is evident that you possess a preference for visiting a marketplace that offers a diverse range of merchandise. This enhances the likelihood of securing the desired product. In this context, it is advisable that you search for an affiliate marketing platform that offers a diverse range of products for promotional purposes. This is likely to lead to an increased availability of products within your selected market segment. This enhances your blogging venture by allowing you to effectively maximize revenue streams from your content, while also presenting a diverse range of products for your audience to select from.

Variety in sources of revenue "

The variability of revenue sources is predominantly contingent upon:

The assortment of products provided by a specific affiliate marketing platform directly influences the potential for increased marketing opportunities within your specified niche.

The assorted assortment of promotional advertisements available for each specific product in the affiliate program. Certain affiliate marketing platforms solely provide in-text hyperlinks. Additionally, certain alternatives provide textual content alongside animated hyperlinks, whereas others incorporate video links as a supplementary feature to the aforementioned choices. The more extensive the range of alternatives available, the simpler it becomes to optimize your content and affiliate links. Each of these aforementioned variants of affiliate advertisements represents a distinct source of revenue, as it is likely that a potential customer who may have refrained from clicking on an inline hyperlink would be inclined to click on either a video advertisement or an animated flash advertisement instead.

Payment terms

The paramount significance lies in the capability to convert one's affiliate earnings into monetary funds. Certain affiliate marketing platforms impose restrictions when it comes to withdrawing your earnings. Certain individuals strongly advocate for making a direct bank transfer solely to a local bank situated within the jurisdiction of the platform, such as exclusively to a

United States bank. In addition to direct bank transfer, certain parties provide the option of check payment. There exists a cohort of individuals who possess sufficient adaptability to provide alternative payment options through email, such as PayPal and Skrill.

In addition to your capacity to convert your affiliate earnings into cash, it is imperative to acquaint yourself with the frequency at which you can make withdrawals and the minimum threshold for withdrawal. The majority of affiliate marketing platforms establish a specific minimum withdrawal threshold, which typically falls within the range of $20 to $100. However, certain restrictions exist regarding the frequency of withdrawals, as some institutions only permit withdrawals on a weekly or bi-monthly basis, for instance. Please verify the payment terms to prevent acquiring benefits that cannot be enjoyed.

Terms of service

The terms of service hold utmost importance in your selection of an affiliate marketing platform. It is imperative that you read with great attention to the finer intricacies. Don't overlook any detail. Certain terms of service on certain affiliate marketing platforms have zero tolerance for violations. This could result in significant financial penalties or the complete deactivation of your account. Therefore, it is advised that you carefully review the terms of service prior to making a commitment to a specific affiliate marketing platform.

The most renowned affiliate marketing platforms.

Over the course of time, specific marketing platforms have demonstrated remarkable resilience and advancement, ultimately establishing themselves as the preferred choices for the majority of product merchants and affiliate marketers.

Here is a list of the leading affiliate marketing platforms for you to consider as a preliminary selection while you further examine each platform in relation to the specific niche you are targeting.

Commission junction

Clickbank

ShareAsale

Linkshare

Amazon Associates

In contrast to alternative models, Amazon Associates uniquely concentrates its attention solely on merchandise available for purchase within the Amazon marketplace. As such, it can be regarded as an affiliate platform primarily influenced by merchants. It is considered the foremost choice when it comes to marketing products that are already part of the Amazon platform. Nevertheless, if you are not currently engaged in marketing products via the Amazon platform, it is imperative to take into account the aforementioned four platforms.

Fundamentals of Affiliate Marketing

Prior to delving into the commonly employed terminology in the field of affiliate marketing, it is indispensable to provide you with a comprehensive overview of the fundamental principles and objectives of affiliate marketing. In the event that you are already aware of this information, you may choose to bypass this section and proceed to the following one.

It is not challenging to commence

One of the primary rationales behind the widespread popularity of affiliate marketing lies in its inherent simplicity, which renders it accessible to virtually anyone interested in embarking on this venture. No proficiency in the field is required to become an associate marketer, and you can commence your journey with a minimal investment. We acknowledge that you may not currently require a website, however, we highly recommend that you consider making an investment in one. The cost for a domain name is estimated to be approximately $10 per annum, in addition to the necessity of a web hosting account. Website hosting typically comes with a monthly fee ranging from $5 to $15, and it is necessary in order to make your website accessible on the Internet.

Numerous individuals forgo the creation of their own website due to perceiving it as excessively challenging. This statement is false as one may avail themselves of the complimentary WordPress blogging platform, while selecting a gratis theme to be employed for the visual and aesthetic aspects of their website. It is remarkably effortless to incorporate newly contented individuals to your website by means of the WordPress platform. After setting up all the necessary components, you can promptly commence generating subsidiary commissions within a remarkably short duration. Numerous digital resources can be found online, such as instructional videos on platforms like YouTube, which provide guidance on initiating a successful affiliate marketing campaign.

One possible alternative in a formal tone could be: "You have the option to exclusively promote your subsidiary proposals through virtual platforms for entertainment, such as Pinterest, Instagram, Facebook, and similar channels." If you follow this approach, there will be no need for you to concern yourself with a website. The problem lies in the fact that exposure on a public platform has the potential to diminish the quality of your content, leaving you devoid of any valuable material.

The progression of affiliate marketing

There are three participants involved in an auxiliary exhibition industry:

The vendor of the merchandise or services (the individual or entity that possesses the goods)

The advertiser, who is a member of our program, promotes the products or services and receives a commission as agreed upon.

The ultimate customer who purchases the product or service

The following aspects are managed by the merchandise or service provider:

• Product or service development

- An effective sales funnel to market the product or service

- Comprehensive client support services

- The arrangement of special partner rats

The strategic placement of promotional tools for affiliates

- Ensuring timely payment of associate commissions

Your responsibility as a derivative is to locate and pursue potential customers for the product or service. You will direct visitor traffic towards the promotions you promote through distinct affiliate rates. The subordinate agents are an exceptional asset that will facilitate seamless communication pertaining to any transactions, ensuring timely receipt of your financial remittances.

The customer is the individual or entity that makes a purchase of the item or service. If they encounter any assistance concerns, they will handle the matter with the merchant. It is highly likely that they will be unaware of the fact that they have made a purchase or availed a service via an affiliate link.

⬚ Training in Affiliate Marketing

Numerous educational courses are available to teach effective strategies for becoming a productive and valued contributor. Some of these options are available at no cost, whereas the superior ones generally require payment. If you are genuinely committed to achieving lasting success in affiliate marketing, it is essential to be prepared to invest in educational programs that will provide valuable guidance. It is essential to procure membership showcasing instructional class from an individual with a commendable track record and reputable stature in the industry. John Crestani is an exemplary individual with an exceptional background and a renowned reputation. He consistently earns a substantial income as a business associate.

John Crestani is widely known for his highly renowned course known as the Super Partner Framework. This is a comprehensive 6-week preparatory program that will equip you with all the necessary knowledge and skills to become a successful participant.

The Super Partner Framework will provide you with the following benefits:

• Gradual progression towards achieving success in affiliate marketing

• Selecting the appropriate specialization.

The most exemplary collaborating entities

• Searching for the most promising proposals to promote

• Key pitfalls to steer clear of in affiliate marketing • Common blunders to be mindful of when engaging in affiliate marketing • Errors to circumvent in the realm of affiliate marketing

- Online platforms and digital marketing strategies for generating sales

- Effective methods for generating targeted website traffic (utilizing search engine optimization, leveraging YouTube, implementing solo advertisements, integrating virtual entertainment, and more)

- Advertising campaigns that advocate

- The record of million-dollar transfers, wherein John presents you with his pre-established successful affiliate assignments.

Successfully executed for your channel pages

A individualized teleconference with Mr. John Crestani

- Access granted to the enigmatic locale imbued with assistance and reinforcement

And significantly more...

John Crestani's knowledge and expertise in running successful affiliate marketing campaigns is comprehensive and extensive. The Super Partner Framework has garnered extensive praise from satisfied clients, positioning it as the premier affiliate marketing training program available.

In the subsequent section, we will explore the most commonly employed terminology in affiliate marketing...

Enhancing Marketing Strategies to Drive Sales and Maximize Profitability

As an affiliate marketer, it has become evident that the adage, "consistently maintain an active marketing approach," aptly applies to you. In order to disseminate information regarding the arrangements you are marketing, it is necessary to communicate and engage in promotional activities.

Fortunately, a range of cost-effective promotional strategies are available to promote your affiliate business, some of which require only your time investment. It is important to bear in mind that aside from your primary product or service, there may be other aspects of your business that require marketing attention.

You are advised to promote your proprietary affiliate program to those individuals who seek financial gain. It is advisable to promote and advertise the products you develop or discover to the individuals who require them. In light of this, it is imperative to distinctly market business-to-business and business-to-customer interactions, treating them as distinct entities that should be kept separate from one another.

You can employ congruent marketing strategies, although the messaging and presentation will vary based on the target demographic and the product being promoted. Content marketing is the foremost means to promote your business.

• Content Marketing

This particular marketing approach encompasses all forms of content-driven marketing, including social media marketing, blogging, and email marketing. Establish a plan for every individual item that requires promotion. Take into consideration the intended audience, the platform on which the content will be displayed, and the appropriate source of inspiration.

•Search Engine Optimization

Acquire knowledge about SEO given its crucial role in your success. It will assist in the improvement of your titles and headlines, leading to enhanced accuracy in targeting and undoubtedly resulting in heightened happiness.

Please bear in mind that SEO encompasses a range of on-page and off-page strategies - from internal link building to obtaining external backlinks, and all aspects should be duly considered. Incorporating programming such as Yoast SEO into your blog can provide substantial assistance.

• Paid Marketing

The most effective affiliate marketers employ paid advertising in addition to the available free alternatives. Nevertheless, it is important to bear in mind that genuine freedom of choice does not exist. You will have to either allocate your personal time or expend your own financial resources. The choice you make is contingent upon your needs and abilities.

• Social Media Marketing

Ensure the comprehensive development of each platform that is utilized in order to articulate and project your brand voice and desired image onto the global stage. Employ the material you create to disseminate information to the general population consistently, employing both complimentary and remunerated methods.

• Email Marketing

Email marketing holds significant importance in content marketing, however, it is crucial to emphasize that overlooking email marketing is not a viable option for long-term success as an affiliate advertiser. Establishing and nurturing a personalized subscriber list, based on your target audience's preferences, is the key to sustaining a prosperous business amidst the evolving dynamics of your desired demographic and the transient nature of social media platforms.

• Affiliates

In accordance with our prior discussion, it has been suggested that the implementation of your own affiliate program could prove beneficial in terms of marketing and selling the products developed by you, keeping in mind the specific needs of your target audience. This is an excellent strategy for creating excitement and disseminating information more expeditiously about any product you manufacture.

Upon acquiring ownership of your products, initiate the process of accepting affiliates. Start by reaching out to your most satisfied clientele and providing them with the necessary training to become profitable affiliates for your business.

• Joint Venture Partnerships

An effective strategy for promoting your business involves forging strategic alliances with individuals or entities that cater to the same target audience as you, offering complementary products and services. By chance, these circumstances provide opportunities for you to promote their products as an affiliate and vice versa.

In a joint venture, two or more parties agree to collaborate towards a mutual objective, either temporarily or over an extended period, while maintaining separate business entities except for the joint venture itself.

As an illustration, it is possible to establish connections and foster relationships with numerous acquaintances through the utilization of affiliate programs. These programs provide various opportunities for working mothers with young children, such as engagements involving meal planning, family management, personal growth, and a plethora of other possibilities.

One option could be: "A webinar could be organized, featuring one or two local experts who would each present their respective products or services to the audience." All individuals collectively engage in marketing the event concurrently to generate excitement. Subsequently, the webinar can be streamed in real-time, and one can even opt to replay it in a live simulcast fashion, thereby generating a substantially higher number of potential leads.

The most effective approach to increasing business transactions and reaping rewards is to enhance marketing efforts. Increase stakeholder engagement and ensure extensive discourse around your products and services by mobilizing a larger number of individuals. Please do not hesitate to enthusiastically inform your audience about your offerings. Taking everything into account, one discerns their efficacy and is satisfied with them. Why would you not provide individuals with as much information as possible on the matter?

Exploring Lucrative Affiliate Programs

Choose the profitable tool for your chosen business sector.

You can decide in 2 different ways.

Choose an affiliate program or
Join an affiliate network and analyze them individually.

A trader hires affiliates through an affiliate framework in an affiliate program. The vendor will directly collaborate with the affiliates. No external parties are allowed for discussion. The vendor will distribute affiliate links, provide support for promoting products, and ultimately pay affiliate bonuses.

An affiliate network is a platform that affiliates can join. He will gain access to numerous products from various merchants upon selection. He has the choice to select the product for advertising. The affiliate network acts as the intermediary between the affiliates and the vendors. Every decision has pros and cons. Choosing an affiliate network is ideal for those who struggle to decide on a specific product to promote. Affiliate networks provide abundant opportunities for potential affiliate marketers, with a wide array of product choices and complete autonomy in decision-making.

The issue?

Numerous individuals share the same contemplated affiliate networks. There are countless competitors for any product you choose within an affiliate network. Online success is easily achievable. Maximize profit by minimizing competition through mathematical statement.

This applies to all businesses. If countless affiliates market a hot product via affiliate networks, your chances of success will greatly decrease. Enrollment in an affiliate network doesn't imply failure. You will improve and succeed in affiliate marketing despite competition as you progress in the lessons.

Now, let's move on to affiliate programs. Fewer products for advertising will be available from an affiliate program, obviously. You'll only have access to the merchant's products. However, affiliate programs employ fewer affiliates. This implies less competition. This also leads to greater chances for success. Unsatisfied with the sales of a particular product through an affiliate program? No issue!

No limit exists for joining multiple affiliate programs. All member programs can join, making it even more terrific. Your enrollment comes at no cost, not even a single penny. Ultimately, you will be assisting the vendor in selling his products. You are the payee! Currently, there are good affiliate programs and bad member programs. How can you identify which to avoid?

Stay alert for the following indicators:

Selling a low-quality product. This low-quality product will generate refund requests due to its inability to meet a need. Referring some orders could reduce your bonus due to the refunds. You risk losing credibility with potential customers by directing them towards a poor product.
Providing a challenging product to offer. This is self- informative. You won't

understand your payments if the product you're preselling is a difficult offer.

The program has a track record of not paying affiliates. Frustration arises when efforts go unrewarded.

The affiliate program has a questionable track record in customer and partner management.

The affiliate network is struggling financially.

The affiliate network is managed by anonymous individuals.

If you encounter an affiliate program possessing any of these qualities, avoid it. How do you currently prioritize the correct affiliate program? Ultimately, the ideal affiliate project should possess most, if not all, of these qualities:

A hot-offering product. This is currently my top concern. Without preselling any products, I can't win as a member, right? Therefore, I typically seek programs with products of proven value in a specific industry, or at least, products with substantial potential.

Gratuitous commission plan. This is merely optional for the aforementioned variable. My base commission rate is 50%. Anything less requires more focus. Most member programs now offer 50% commission for every sale, so this shouldn't be a problem.

A widely recognized program with a high level of believability. Who would require association with glimmer in the skillet, temporary stations, correct? Must you become a champion? Stay loyal to a winner! Rely on advice and diligent efforts to find an affiliate program.

Excellent customer support for a program. Discount solicitations are the enemies in affiliate advertising. If a refund is requested later, no commission will be received despite your initial belief of making a sale.

A program with excellent customer support reduces demands and guarantees game protection.

For affiliate networking, www.cj.com, www.linkshare.com, and www.clickbank.com are excellent starting points. They offer an exceptional range of products with generous commissions.

3. Studying knowledge
Knowledge research is the next step after selecting a niche and finding a good number of keywords. The topic is easily understood from its name.

Consider these aspects for Knowledge Research.

Learn more about the niche.

Do extensive niche research, regardless of your opinions.

I spent approximately one week researching my current niche, and it continues to be beneficial. It is beneficial when someone seeks advice within my expertise.

It aids in writing an article, enabling you to express your opinions about the discussed product.

You must research Gym Supplements if you start working on that niche.

What ingredients are in gym supplements? What components are included?

Key factors to consider when purchasing gym supplements, potential pitfalls to avoid, recommended dosage, and possible side effects.

Despite not having used the exact product, these things enable you to express relevant opinions in your article. This is a great demonstration of conducting research for a specific niche.

Key vocabulary for your niche

The terms mentioned pertain to the niche of digital cameras and DSLRs.

Understanding terminology is crucial in every niche, as it defines their meaning, purpose, and function.

If you don't learn these terms, you'll receive many comments criticizing your lack of knowledge.

Also, it is beneficial when your website gains authority in its niche and people seek your advice on different products through comments or social media.

Popular Products

Apple iPhone is popular in the smartphone market or Rolex is a well-known luxury watch brand.

You must be aware of popular products in your niche. That's it. No other option.

You can utilize Wikipedia, Amazon Best Sellers, niche related forums, niche related authority sites, and user reviews.

Comparing the product with a popular one in the niche aids in writing reviews. Prior to proceeding to the next topic, here's a brief overview on the importance of Research before beginning a niche.

Research is crucial before starting an Amazon niche site as it can determine its success or failure. The root empowers your entire website's existence.

Without improvement, achieving $1000/month will remain a distant dream. Some bloggers aim to create a successful blog but fail to make significant profits. Why?

Due to insufficient research capabilities, numerous bloggers who start multiple blogs fail and do not earn substantial income from them. Thorough research ensures intelligence amidst a sea of uninformed bloggers.

I recognized this and thus dedicated 2 months solely to researching my niche, enabling me to achieve my goal of $1000/month within 5 months of blog inception. Isn't that cool? Yes, it is.

Alright! Now, it's time to focus on the captivating and crucial aspect of constructing an Authority Amazon Niche Site.

Shall we start?

Chapter 2: Earning from Your Website

All types of websites, whether personal blogs, news sites, or company websites, can be monetized through various channels. Each website must find the ideal monetization channels that work best for them.

To assess your website's effectiveness, use A/B testing with Optimizely or heat mapping with CrazyEgg. A/B testing determines the most effective layout for optimizing monetization strategies on your website by testing different layouts with content and ads and analyzing customer engagement rates. Choose frequency for each site version, receive report on highest engagement rate.

Heat mapping shows a screenshot of your site with red to blue spots indicating areas of high or low engagement. Some information may be surprising and go against your assumptions.

Maximizing website engagement is crucial for monetization. Optimize through proper placement.

Advertising

Many people immediately consider putting digital display ads on their website to monetize it. Ads are uploaded to your site using slot tokens and keywords for contextual display on your site. Ads are typically targeted based on user demographics and search history, or they may be relevant to the website the user is viewing.

PPC and CTR are used in digital advertising. Advertisers pay for each click on the ad; higher CTR equals better ad performance and more earnings.

Do not use Google AdSense on your new website within the first six months as they may penalize and potentially block you from using AdSense. It is challenging to utilize AdSense and achieve desired click-through rates due to the numerous terms and conditions involved.

Email Marketing

Email marketing monetizes websites effectively. Specific email lists enable you to send precisely desired content to the interested audience. They want to see it because they opted to receive a specific newsletter via email from your website. Email lists are crucial for increasing website traffic and monetizing your site.

Increasing email subscribers demonstrates to marketing or advertising companies that your website has reach and can be utilized for promoting products to the subscribers' enjoyment. Subscribed readers trust sender and their opinions in email marketing.

Subscribe to the newsletter.

You can promote products and services to them easily through paid sponsorship or affiliate marketing, and they trust you more than pesky ads.

Email marketing service providers can assist you in creating campaigns, managing email lists, and tracking campaign performance by providing information on open rates, click-through rates, and overall engagement. Knowing website performance and audience interaction is crucial. Utilize this data to enhance your monetization channels.

Paid Sponsorship

Paid sponsorship monetizes your website by companies paying you to sponsor their product or service on your website. A sponsor will compensate you for writing about their product, dedicating a section on your website to their product, or paying for an ad space. They pay you to advertise their message, product, or services on your blog, hoping for conversions.

Sponsorship can be non-monetary, instead they provide you the product or service free of charge. They might offer complimentary hotel stays in exchange for a review on your website. Sponsor payment is based on website traffic, social media followers, and email subscribers.

Sell items: eBooks & courses

Every website and blog has a specific audience. Your website likely won't succeed without a niche. Being a niche expert ensures repeated visits for further learning. Courses and eBooks establish authority, trust, and assist in branding.

Providing valuable material to readers via courses and eBooks demonstrates extensive knowledge and can generate income. People are likely to purchase an eBook or enroll in a course on a specific subject or new topic. People enjoy using their free time to learn and browse the

Internet for new reading material. You can earn income by selling your eBook on your website and allowing other websites to link and sell your eBook too.

Affiliate Marketing

Affiliate marketing reimburses for clicks resulting in purchases, unlike paid sponsorships. You can monetize your website immediately with affiliate marketing. Implement affiliate marketing immediately on your website and wait for the income to start, though it is advised to create some content before applying affiliate marketing.

Affiliate marketing companies may approach you if your blog or website receives good traffic and request to be added. You can also join various networks like JVZoo, ClickBank, Amazon, and CJ Affiliate.

These networks have numerous merchants and a vast range of products to choose from. Find the product, get your unique ID link, then place it on your website. This link directs customers to the merchant's website for product purchase. The merchant knows the sale came from you and you will receive the commission through the affiliate marketing network where you got the link.